I WONDER WHY

Stars Twinkle

KINGFISHER
LONDON & NEW YORK

LONDON & NEW YORK

Copyright © Macmillan Publishers International Ltd 2011, 2023
Published in the United States by Kingfisher
120 Broadway, New York, NY 10271
Kingfisher is a division of Macmillan Children's Books, London

ISBN: 978-0-7534-7926-1 (HB)
ISBN: 978-0-7534-7925-4 (PB)

Distributed in the U.S. and Canada by Macmillan,
120 Broadway, New York, NY 10271

EU representative: Macmillan Publishers Ireland Ltd,
1st Floor, The Liffey Trust Centre,
117-126 Sheriff Street Upper, Dublin 1, D01 YC43.

Library of Congress Cataloging-in-Publication
data has been applied for.

Author: Carole Stott
Consultant: Dr David Hughes

2023 edition
Editor: Seeta Parmar
Designer: Peter Clayman
Design Assistant: Amelia Brooks
Illustrator: Marie-Eve Tremblay

Kingfisher books are available for special
promotions and premiums. For details contact:
Special Markets Department, Macmillan,
120 Broadway, New York, NY 10271.

For more information, please visit
www.kingfisherbooks.com.

Printed in China
9 8 7 6 5 4 3 2 1
1TR/0723/WKT/RV/128MA

FSC
www.fsc.org
MIX
Paper | Supporting
responsible forestry
FSC® C116313

CONTENTS

What is the universe?

The **whole world and everything** beyond it is the universe. It is all the stars and planets, Earth, and its plants and animals, you and me —everything.

No one knows where all the material to make the universe came from in the first place.

The big bang explosion sent the young universe flying out in all directions. Over very long periods of time, parts came together to make galaxies.

There are huge groups of stars in space. They are called galaxies, and they're like gigantic star cities.

When did it all begin?

Many astronomers think that everything in the universe was once packed together in one small lump. Then, about 14 billion years ago, there was a gigantic **explosion** called the **big bang.**

The galaxies are still speeding apart today, and the universe is getting bigger.

You are made of the same stuff as a star!

Will the universe ever end?

Some **astronomers** think the universe will just carry on getting bigger as the galaxies speed apart. Others think that the galaxies may one day start falling back toward each other until they crash together in a **big crunch**! Astronomers are scientists who study the stars and the planets.

What is the Milky Way?

The Milky Way is the **galaxy** we live in. It is made up of all the stars you can see in the sky at night, and **many, many more** you cannot see.

The Milky Way is a barred spiral galaxy. Below you can see what it looks like from above—a little like a whirlpool with long, spiraling arms.

We live on a planet called Earth, which travels around a star called the Sun.

SUN

EARTH

There are four main galaxy shapes. The barred spiral is one. Here are the others:

The Milky Way got its name because at night we can sometimes see part of it looking like a band of milky white light across the sky.

IRREGULAR (NO SPECIAL SHAPE)

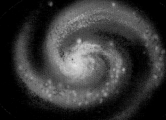

ELLIPTICAL (EGG-SHAPED)

SPIRAL

How many stars are there?

There are at least **100 billion stars** in the Milky Way. That is nearly 13 stars for every person living on Earth today! Although we cannot see all of it, astronomers have worked out how big the **universe** is and how many stars it might have. There are about **10 thousand billion** stars in around 100 billion galaxies. It is hard to imagine so many stars, let alone count them all!

Astronomers usually give galaxies numbers instead of names. Only a few have names that tell us what they look like—the Whirlpool, the Sombrero, and the Black Eye, for example.

What are stars made of?

Stars are not solid like the ground beneath your feet. Instead, they are made of **gases** like the air around you. The two main gases in stars are hydrogen and helium. They are the stars' **fuel**. Stars make heat and light from them.

Since ancient times, stargazers have seen patterns in the way stars are grouped in the sky. These patterns are called constellations.

SIRIUS

The brightest star we can see in the night sky is called Sirius. Another name for it is the Dog Star. It is about twice as big as our Sun, but it gives out more than 20 times as much light!

Why do stars twinkle?

Stars twinkle only when we look at them from Earth. Out in space, their **light** shines steadily. We see them twinkling and shimmering because of the **air** around Earth—as light from a star travels toward us, it is bent and wobbled by bubbles of hot and cold air.

Light bends when it passes through different things. If you put a pencil in a glass of water, for example, it looks bent because it is half in air and half in water.

Are stars star-shaped?

No, stars are **round** like balls. We give them pointed edges when we draw them because this is what they look like from Earth, with their light **blinking** and **twinkling**.

What is a red giant?

All stars are born, live for a very long time, and then die. A red giant is a **huge, ancient star**.

1 All stars are born in huge spinning clouds of gas and dust. Our Sun was born 4.6 billion years ago.

2 The gas and dust come together to make lots of balls, which become star clusters.

3 Most stars are like our Sun and shine steadily for almost all their lives.

4 Toward the end of their lives, stars like our Sun swell up and become as much as 100 times bigger. They turn into red giants. Our Sun will do this in about five billion years.

5 When it has used up all its gas fuel, a red giant shrinks down into a white dwarf. It is then about 10,000 times smaller but still very hot.

If you think of our Sun as shining like a car's headlights, then a red giant would shine like a lighthouse!

On Earth, a sugar-lump-sized piece of a white dwarf would weigh as much as a small car!

6 The star cools down and ends its life billions of years later, as a black dwarf—a cold, black cinder.

Which stars explode?

Different kinds of stars lead different lives. Some stars have a lot more gas fuel in them than others. These really **massive stars** do not die quietly by cooling down. Instead, they blow up in a huge flash of light. Stars that explode like this are called **supernovae**.

Stars must have at least eight times as much gas fuel as our Sun to end their lives in supernova explosions.

What is a black hole?

A black hole can happen when a massive star dies. The star falls in on itself, **squashing** all its material and becoming smaller and smaller. In the end, all that is left is a place from which light cannot escape—**a black hole**. Everything in space has a pulling force called **gravity**—galaxies, stars, planets like Earth, and even moons. Gravity holds things together and stops them from **floating** away into space . . .

Light is sucked into black holes in much the same way as water is sucked down a drain.

A star that gets too close to a black hole is sucked into it. Nothing, not even the star's light, can escape the pull of the black hole's gravity.

. . . But stars that become black holes have **very strong** gravity—that is what **pulls them inward** and makes them collapse.

When two large space bodies (such as a planet and a moon) get close enough, there is a pulling competition between their forces of gravity. It is like a giant tug of war.

A planet's gravity holds its moons close to it and stops them from shooting off into space.

However high you jump, Earth's gravity stops you from floating.

How hot is the Sun?

Like all stars, our Sun is a huge ball of **super-hot gas**. It is hottest in the middle—the temperature there is around **27 million °F** (15 million °C). The outside of the Sun is a lot cooler than the middle—only 10,000°F (5,500°C). But this is still much, much hotter than the hottest oven!

Dark patches called sunspots come and go on the face of the Sun. They make it look as if it has the chickenpox. Sunspots are dark because they are cooler and so give out less light than the rest of the Sun. Most sunspots are larger than Earth!

The ancient Greeks believed that the Sun was a god called Helios. He rode across the sky in a chariot of flames.

Plants and animals could not live without the Sun's heat and light.

The Sun is the only star that is close enough to Earth for us to feel its heat. The next closest star to Earth is called Proxima Centauri. Our Sun's light takes 8.3 minutes to reach us, but Proxima Centauri's takes 4.3 years!

Will the Sun ever go out?

One day, the Sun will **use up** all its gas fuel and die. But this will not happen in your lifetime, or your children's, or even your great-great-great grandchildren's! Astronomers think that the Sun has enough gas fuel to last for at least another **five billion years**.

The Sun uses more than 30 million truckloads of fuel every second!

How many planets are there?

PLUTO

Pluto used to be classified as a planet, but is now known as a dwarf planet.

Our planet, Earth, has seven **neighbors**. Together they make a family of eight main planets that travel around the **Sun**. We call the Sun, and all the space bodies that whirl around it, the **solar system**. Besides the Sun and the planets, the solar system includes moons, dwarf planets, asteroids, and comets.

The word planet *comes from the Greek word* planetes, *which means "wanderer."*

URANUS

JUPITER

NEPTUNE

SATURN

Millions of asteroids orbit the Sun in a belt between Mars and Jupiter. Some are like grains of sand. Others are as big as houses. A few are the size of Pennsylvania!

COMET

Comets are rather like huge dirty snowballs. Most stay on the edge of the solar system, but a few travel close to the Sun. These comets grow gas and dust tails millions of miles long when the Sun's heat starts to melt them.

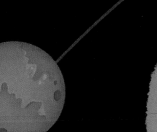

MARS

What is the difference between planets and stars?

Planets are not as **big** or as **hot** as stars, and they cannot make their own light. They were made from the leftovers of the same **gas** and **dust** cloud that gave birth to our star, the Sun.

EARTH

SUN

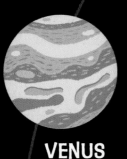

VENUS

MERCURY

An orbit is the path of a planet around the Sun, or a moon around a planet. The planets all have different orbits. Mercury is the closest planet to the Sun.

Why is Earth so special?

Our planet is the only one in the solar system with flowing **liquid water** and living things on it. That makes it very special. It is the third planet from the Sun, and it gets just the right amount of **heat** and **light** to keep us alive. Any closer, and it would be too hot. Any farther away, and it would be too cold.

About 71% of the Earth's surface is covered by water.

When the Sun turns into a red giant star, it will swallow up Mercury and get so large that it will cover half of our midday sky.

Astronomers think that millions of stars in the universe have families of planets. They have discovered more than 70 solar systems and are finding more all the time.

Why does the Sun go out at night?

It gets dark at night because Earth is **spinning** as it orbits the Sun. As parts of Earth spin away from the Sun, they move out of its light and into **darkness**. It takes a whole day and night for Earth to spin around once.

All planets spin as they orbit the Sun.

You can see what happens as Earth spins if you turn a globe in the beam of light from a flashlight.

Which is the hottest planet?

Venus is not the closest planet to the Sun, but it is the **hottest**. The temperature there can reach 870°F (465°C). For comparison, the highest temperature ever recorded on Earth was **136°F (58°C)**, in Al'Aziziyah in the Libyan Desert, North Africa.

Space probes have landed on Venus and sent back pictures and information to Earth. The probes were destroyed soon after landing, however, by the super-hot climate on Venus.

Although Mercury (right) is closer to the Sun, Venus is hotter! This is because Venus is covered by thick clouds of gas that act like a blanket, trapping the Sun's heat.

Mercury is covered in craters—hollows made by huge space rocks crashing into it. If you could visit Mercury, you would see that the Sun looks more than twice as big there as it does from Earth. This is because Mercury is so much closer to the Sun.

Which is the red planet?

Mars is often called the **red planet**. The ground there is covered in dusty red soil that gets swept up by the wind to make pink clouds! The rocks on Mars have a lot of **iron** in them, and iron turns red when it **rusts**. A better name for Mars might be the rusty planet!

Living things need water. If there is any on Mars, it is frozen inside the planet's north and south polar icecaps.

Mars is the next planet from the Sun after ours, and people once thought that, like Earth, it might have living things. Space probes have been visiting, and have found clues that there may once have been life there.

Which is the biggest planet?

Jupiter is so huge that all the other planets could fit inside it! The **beautiful patterns** on its face are made by swirling clouds of **gas**, stirred up by **powerful** wind storms.

The planets Jupiter, Saturn, Uranus, and Neptune are called the gas giants. They are all very big, and they are mainly made of gas, with small, rocky centers.

Jupiter is one of four planets with rings around them.

JUPITER

Jupiter's Great Red Spot is so big that two Earths could fit inside it! It is a gigantic storm that has been raging for more than 300 years.

GREAT RED SPOT

Jupiter was named by the ancient Romans, after the king of their gods.

Astronomers send telescopes into space, because the air around Earth stops some of the light and other information from stars and planets from reaching us. The James Webb Space Telescope was launched in 2021. It can almost see to the edge of the universe!

JAMES WEBB SPACE TELESCOPE

SATURN

SATURN'S RINGS

Many people think that Saturn's glistening rings make it the most beautiful planet in the solar system. Pictures sent back to Earth by space probes have shown us that the rings are made up of ice, rock, and dust.

Which planet is furthest from the Sun?

Neptune is the most **distant** and the coldest main planet. But beyond Neptune are at least a thousand icy rock bodies called **Kuiper Belt Objects**, as well as the dwarf planet Pluto.

On Neptune, the temperature is an incredibly icy –330°F (–200°C). Even ice cream would taste as hot as soup on this planet.

Which planet is tipped over?

Uranus is the sideways planet. Its **moons** and **rings** go around its middle— but because it is on its side, they look as if they circle it from top to toe. Uranus was not always like this. It got knocked over by a **huge asteroid** when it was young.

How do we know about the furthest planets?

Until the American *Voyager 2* **spacecraft** visited Uranus in 1986 and Neptune in 1989, not a lot was known about these planets. *Voyager 2* gave us our first **close-up** look at these two distant worlds. The spacecraft's cameras showed us 16 of Uranus's moons and eight of Neptune's. Since then, more have been discovered using Earth's most **powerful telescopes**. Now we know that Neptune has 14 moons and Uranus has 27.

Voyager 2 left Earth in 1977 and reached Neptune 12 years later, in 1989.

Which planet has the biggest moons?

Moons are rocky bodies that orbit (circle) planets. Jupiter has at least 80 moons, and three of them—**Ganymede**, **Callisto**, and **Io**—are larger than Earth's moon. Mercury and Venus are the only planets that do not have moons. All the other planets have at least one.

CALLISTO

OUR MOON

GANYMEDE

IO

In pictures taken by the space probe Voyager 2, Io looks like a giant cheese pizza. The red color comes from volcanoes.

Which planet's moons look like potatoes?

If Earth were the size of an orange, then the Moon would be the size of a cherry.

Mars has two tiny moons that look like lumpy old potatoes. They are called **Deimos** and **Phobos**, and unlike larger moons, they are not round.

What is it like on our Moon?

Earth's Moon is **dry**, **dusty**, and **lifeless**. There is no air to breathe or water to drink. During the day, it is so hot that your blood would boil. At night, it is **freezing cold**—not a nice place to take a vacation!

On July 20, 1969, two American astronauts became the first people ever to set foot on the Moon. Their names were Neil Armstrong and Buzz Aldrin, and their space mission was called Apollo 11.

The Moon's gravity is weaker than Earth's. You would be much lighter on the Moon— only one-sixth of your Earth weight. So you would be able to jump six times as high!

How fast do space rockets go?

Rockets have to **travel faster** than 7 miles (11km) per second to get into space. This works out to about **25,000 miles per hour** (40,000km/h)—and car drivers can get into trouble for speeding at 70 miles per hour (110km/h)! If rockets did not travel so fast, they would not be able to escape the enormously strong pull of Earth's gravity.

The tallest rocket ever launched was Saturn V, which took the Apollo 11 spacecraft into space and the first people to the Moon. It was more than 330 feet (100m) tall.

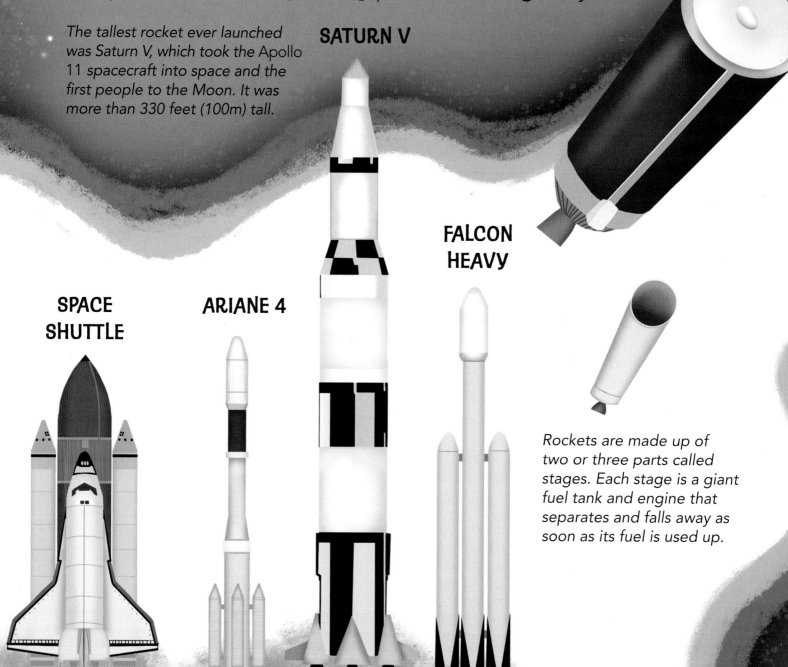

SATURN V

FALCON HEAVY

SPACE SHUTTLE

ARIANE 4

Rockets are made up of two or three parts called stages. Each stage is a giant fuel tank and engine that separates and falls away as soon as its fuel is used up.

At the top of a rocket is its payload—a satellite, a robotic space probe, or a spacecraft carrying astronauts.

New rockets such as the Falcon rockets built by SpaceX are designed to be mostly reusable. After delivering their payloads in space, they land back on Earth to be used again.

What are rockets used for?

Rockets are mostly used to put machines called **satellites** into orbit around Earth. Different kinds of satellites are **launched** to do many different jobs.

Navigation satellites help ships and aircraft to find their way.

Communications satellites pick up and send TV and telephone signals.

Some satellites help us to work out what the weather will be like.

Why do astronauts wear space suits?

There is **no air** to breathe in space, and depending on whether a spacecraft is in or out of the Sun's light, it's either very hot or very cold. Without space suits to **protect** them outside their spacecraft, astronauts would die.

The gold visors on their helmets protect the astronauts' eyes from the Sun's harmful rays.

On their backs they wear a life-support unit. This provides oxygen for the astronauts to breathe and pumps cooled liquid around their space suits to keep them at the right temperature.

Why do astronauts float in space?

Gravity is everywhere. But **astronauts** on a spacecraft orbiting Earth do not experience it in the same way. The craft and astronauts are **farther away** from the pull of Earth's gravity, so they are actually "falling around" Earth rather than down toward it.

Space stretches you— astronauts can come back to Earth as much as 2 inches (5cm) taller!

Astronauts have to wear seat belts to stop them from floating away, and the difference in gravity makes mealtimes a lot more exciting!

INDEX